BRITAIN IN OLD PHO

Around Hayes & West Drayton

A THIRD SELECTION

PHILIP SHERWOOD

SUTTON PUBLISHING

Sutton Publishing Limited
Phoenix Mill · Thrupp · Stroud
Gloucestershire · GL5 2BU

First published in 2002

Reprinted in 2002

Copyright © Hayes and Harlington Local
History Society and West Drayton and
District Local History Society, 2002

Title page: Workers at Wild & Robbins' van
works, early 1900s.

British Library Cataloguing in Publication Data
A catalogue record for this book is available from the
British Library.

ISBN 0-7509-2768-2

Typeset in 10.5/13.5 Photina.
Typesetting and origination by
Sutton Publishing Limited.
Printed and bound in England by
J.H. Haynes & Co. Ltd, Sparkford.

Philip Sherwood has long family connections with Harlington and Harmondsworth. He is an active member of several amenity and environmental groups, the Publications Editor of the Hayes and Harlington Local History Society and Chairman of the local branch of the Council for the Protection of Rural England. He has edited two previous publications in this series *Around Hayes and West Drayton In Old Photographs* (1996) and *Around Hayes and West Drayton: A Second Selection* (1998). In a related series, he is also author of *Heathrow: 2000 Years of History* (1999).

CONTENTS

Map of the approximate area covered by the book (see facing page). It has been compiled from two ordnance maps produced in the mid-1930s, originally on a scale of 2½ in to the mile. By the time that the map was surveyed most of Hayes and Yiewsley had already been intensively industrialised, but the map shows that the other villages to the south still retained their separate, individual identities. The small area marked 'AIRPORT' at the southern extremity was the private aerodrome of the Fairey Aviation Co. at Heathrow. This was appropriated under false pretences in 1944, and led to the development of Heathrow Airport, which has been aptly described as the 'most disastrous planning blunder to hit our country'. What appears on the map as open land, which at that time was under intensive agricultural use, has now been almost completely urbanised and blighted by the malign presence of the airport.

INTRODUCTION

T his book is the third in a series of old photograph books on the area around Hayes and West Drayton. The previous books are no longer available, but like them, this volume covers that part of the London Borough of Hillingdon which, until 1965, came under the jurisdiction of the Hayes and Harlington Urban District Council (UDC) and the Yiewsley and West Drayton UDC. The district now forms the southernmost part of the borough.

The pictures for the most part cover the period 1900–2000, but the book also includes some earlier photographs and line drawings. Care has been taken not to include too many used in the two previous publications, but the opportunity has been taken to include most of those from two earlier books: *Heathrow and District in Times Past* (1979) and *More About Heathrow and District in Times Past* (1983). These were poorly produced and have long been out of print; about one third of the present book is made up of photographs from them.

Most of the earlier views have been copied from old picture postcards. The advent of relatively cheap photography and improved techniques in printing, led many photographers to produce local views that they knew would have a ready market. Cheap postal rates and several daily deliveries meant that postcards were an efficient means of keeping in touch. One of the most common functions of the cards was the exchange of news between members of a scattered family in domestic service at different places. This has meant that there is an extremely good photographic cover, to a high professional standard, for most parts of the country from the early twentieth century.

Other photographs in the book have been taken from private collections and from the collections of the Hayes and Harlington Local History Society and the West Drayton and District Local History Society. These two societies have made a conscious effort to build up collections within their respective areas.

Allowing for the fact that parish boundaries are not rectangular, the approximate area covered by the book is shown in the map on the facing page. The areas marked on the map in capital letters, WEST DRAYTON, HARLINGTON, HARMONDSWORTH, HAYES and YIEWSLEY, denote the five main parishes that form the chapter headings of the book. An attempt has been made to balance the number of photographs for each of these areas, but the coverage is not uniform as it depends on what is available, what has been used before, and it must be admitted, my own preferences as editor.

At the time that the earlier pictures, which form the majority of the book, were taken the populations of the respective areas were about the same size as each other, which of course is reflected in the number of old photographs that are available. Added to which then, as now, photographers concentrated on churches, inns, old buildings and rural scenes; the industrial areas were largely ignored. This gives an emphasis to Harlington and Harmondsworth that is out of proportion to the present-day populations. In the case of Harmondsworth this is exaggerated by the fact that it embraces not only Harmondsworth village, but also the quite distinct (even now) villages of Sipson, Longford and the former hamlet of Heathrow.

P.T. Sherwood
Harlington 2001

A water-colour painting of Botwell, 1821. The rural scene in the south part of Hayes shows where the present Station Road joins Botwell Lane (to the left) and Coldharbour Lane. At the time of the Inclosure Award in 1816 the house in the centre of the picture belonged to Samuel Turner. The house at the right and all the farm buildings on both sides of the road were held freehold or copyhold by John Baptist Shackle. Members of the Shackle family owned a lot of property in the area well into the twentieth century. All the buildings there had gone by 1866, with the exception of the barn on the right of the picture. The pond in the middle distance was still there, although diminished in size. The Shackle family had built a new house, called Redleaf, by 1866 near the site of the one on the right; it survived until replaced by shops in the early 1930s. This area is now the main shopping centre of Hayes. The painting is by an artist called Hedges, about whom little is known.

1

Hayes

The lych-gate, church tower and one of the weatherboarded cottages that adjoined the gate at Church Green, Hayes Town, early 1900s. Church Green was a popular subject with artists and photographers into the 1920s; after which the cottages were demolished and the pond filled in. Before then the scene had changed little in the previous fifty years.

This painting from 1909 shows much the same scene as on the previous page but from further back so as to include more of the cottages. The cottage with a bow-fronted window was a shop.

Another view of Church Green. St Mary's parish church dates from the early thirteenth century, although the tower is fifteenth century and the lych-gate sixteenth century. The cottages were probably late eighteenth or early nineteenth century when weatherboarding construction was common. The railings to the left of the lych-gate belonged to Hayes Court. The village cattle pound was further to the left, out of the picture. The pond has now been filled in and the cottages and Hayes Court have gone.

The lych-gate of Hayes church dates from the sixteenth century and is unique among the churches in west Middlesex. Unfortunately, its future is uncertain as it has been subjected to frequent attacks by mindless vandals.

Another view of Hayes church seen from the other side of the previous illustrations. The building on the right of the picture is Hayes Court (see next page).

Hayes Court. This house, seen from the church tower, adjoined St Mary's churchyard on its south side. Variously known as Court Farm, Hayes Court or Court House, the building almost certainly had had a close connection with the manor of Hayes, although its exact status has yet to be established. The house as it stood (it was demolished in about 1968 and the site is now a car park) was of late eighteenth- or early nineteenth-century construction, although parts of a possibly earlier building, seen towards the right of the picture, may have been incorporated. The unusual octagonal stable, seen on the other side of the courtyard, dated from the early part of the eighteenth century.

Freeman's Lane, just round the corner from the main village street, *c.* 1914. This lane, once called Fleet Lane, was renamed after John Neville Freeman, vicar of Hayes, 1792–1843. Top: the row of brick or weatherboarded cottages was demolished piecemeal from 1959 onwards. The brick house with three chimney pots was once used as a cottage hospital, and the farthest cottage was the scene of the celebrated murder of a man by his wife in 1884. Bottom: the lane as seen from the other end; the single-storey building among the trees on the right was Denston Lodge.

Manor Lodge, Freeman's Lane. This house, the south side of which is shown here, was probably built in the first half of the seventeenth century (Kew Palace, 1631, has very similar gables), although the rear may have been older. It was originally the vicarage, but it was sold by the rector in about 1865 and renamed Manor Lodge. It was then occupied, for about ten years, by Captain E.R. Spearman, JP, and Lady Maria Spearman, daughter of the 5th Earl of Orkney. During the Second World War the house was used as the company headquarters of a local Home Guard battalion. Eventually falling derelict after the war, it was demolished and the site acquired by the Urban District Council and added to Barra Hall Park.

Church Walk, c. 1905, with the parish church of St Mary in the distance. Dr Triplett's school (Church of England), built in 1863, are on the left. The school was demolished in 1969 and a replacement was built not far away. The orchard at the right now forms part of Barra Hall Park.

The village street, c. 1925. In this view, looking north, are Barden Cottage (probably eighteenth century) on the left, then Providence Villas (c. 1880), Craven House (late eighteenth century) and Hayes Town chapel. This was built in 1788–90 but considerably enlarged in 1843. The house with a classical façade (behind the 1924 Trojan van) is Wistowe House, a seventeenth-century building refronted and altered in the early nineteenth century. It was the home, between 1908 and 1914, of B.J. Edwards, a photographic pioneer who had a small works for the production of photographic plates behind the house. This part of Hayes has been less affected by change than other areas in the district, and although Barden Cottage has gone, and the chapel demolished (and replaced by a new congregational church nearby) several other buildings in the old village street remain intact.

This view of the village, c. 1908, is from the south. It shows Hayes Town chapel, built in 1788 and later enlarged, in the centre. On the right are Wistowe House (with a classical façade) and Barden House, then a shop.

The north end of the village street and the corner of Hemmen Lane, c. 1904. The old cottage and the butcher's shop owned by F. Hyde were demolished shortly afterwards and a new shop and house, bearing the legend 'Drayton House, 1905', was built on the site. The small house fronting on to the street is Little Barden House, which had also been a shop in about 1875, but not in 1904, and the three-storey building next to it is Barden House, then and now a shop. Next to Barden House is Wistowe House (see previous page).

Calf, Provision Merchant, Hayes Town, c. 1900, run by Mrs Ann Calf. As well as selling wines and spirits, bread and groceries, this was also the Hayes Town post office. Porch House (demolished by 1915) can just be seen behind the shop.

Although there is no definite evidence that a lord of the manor of Hayes ever lived in this house, the name Manor House has become attached to it. Traces of a moat and discoveries of pottery indicate that a medieval manor house may have occupied the site. This is the only known photograph showing the house before the extensive alterations that took place in about 1862, after which it was occupied by the rector and renamed Rectory Manor House. The house dated from the seventeenth century, but had obviously been altered at other periods. The building was used as a remand home for boys in the 1930s, when the greater part of the east end was destroyed by fire. The remaining part of the house in 2001 is the centre of a small housing estate.

Harvesters in Grassy Meadow in the large field between the present Grange Road and Church Road, *c.* 1900. The building in the background housed the offices of the Hayes UDC, formed in 1904. The field is still here now, remarkably, although the Beck Theatre has taken up much of it, and further developments have been proposed, even though it is in a conservation area. The council-office building was later made part of the Hayes Cottage Hospital, opened in 1898.

The High Road (Uxbridge Road) at the top of Adam and Eve Lane, now Church Road, *c.* 1914. The old Adam and Eve public house (now replaced by a newer building further back from the road) is on the right. The house in the centre, Oakdene, bears the slogan 'Taxation without Representation is Tyranny – Votes for Women'. It was the home of a local suffragette, Mrs Marion Cunningham, in the years before the First World War. It still exists, without the veranda, but its future is uncertain. The pond is now filled in.

Wood End, shown here, *c.* 1905, was a hamlet just to the west of Hayes Town, as the village was known. The principal building was Wood End House, behind the trees to the right. It was built at various periods between about the mid-seventeenth century and early nineteenth century, and in the latter half of the nineteenth century housed a school for young ladies. It later became a lunatic asylum and finally council offices before it was demolished. The road curving to the left (now Grange Road) was once known as Body Snatchers Lane.

Hayes Peace Celebrations. The procession at Wood End, 9 August 1919. Nearly all the buildings shown have now gone. Grange Cottages on the left were demolished in slum clearance, Clark's Rents behind the trees and the Black Horse public house at the right no longer exist.

Cottages in Wood End Green Road, behind the Angel public house. These are mostly of mid-eighteenth-century date, although one has had a Regency veranda added. The shop was a baker's in about 1905 when the picture was taken. Later on it became a butcher's shop and continued so almost until the time that the row was demolished in 1968–9. The house behind the monkey-puzzle tree was reputed to be haunted.

Cottage in West Drayton Road, near Hayes End: one of a number of thatched cottages that still survived in or near Hayes as late as the 1920s. This one, which was probably built on what was the edge of Hillingdon Heath, might have been early eighteenth century or older, although it is difficult to date small buildings of this kind. It was at Goulds Green and stood on the west side of West Drayton Road, just south of the junction with Green Lane. Being near the Uxbridge Road it was chosen as an illustration in *Tramway Trips and Rambles* published in about 1905, as well as being the subject of the postcard shown here, also published in the early 1900s.

The Angel Inn, High Road, Hayes, 1904. An inn of this name is included in the Hayes Inclosure Award of 1814, when the owners were Messrs Thurbin and Gale and the occupier William Church. By 1904 the licensee was Joseph Thomas. A modern public house of the same name, built between the wars, occupies the same site in the Uxbridge Road at Hayes End.

Laburnam Villa (above) and Springwell House (right), Hayes End Road. In the nineteenth century, Hayes End Road was the preferred location of some of the more prosperous residents of Hayes End. At the end of the road was Hayes Park and at the other end was Hayes End House, both of which have since been demolished. In between were some smaller (but still comparatively large) houses such as Laburnam Villa a double-pile mid-nineteenth century house and locally listed. Springwell House, a Grade II listed building, likewise dates from the mid-nineteenth century, although it also incorporates some eighteenth-century work. Both of these houses are still in existence today.

Hayes Park. Robert Willis Blencowe was the owner of this estate at the time of the Hayes Inclosure in 1814. He replaced the old mansion house with the house shown here not long after the inclosure. By 1845 Hayes Park was the seat of Colonel James Grant, who does not appear to have been there very long, since the 1851 census shows that it was by then a private lunatic asylum, under the supervision of William Conolley, MRCS. There were ten patients described as 'Gentlemen', and one peer – Francis Stewart, 11th Earl of Moray. The house remained a lunatic asylum until it was purchased, together with the surrounding parkland, by H.J. Heinz Co. Ltd, who demolished it during the 1960s in order to build a food research centre.

Park Farm, 1905, stood near the site of the moated manor house of Hayes Park Hall, a sub-manor of the chief manor of Hayes. The manor house was tenanted between about 1795 and 1816 by Judge John Heath, notorious for his severe sentences and for having refused a knighthood. Judge Heath Lane was named after him, and the site is where the sports ground is now.

Yeading Lane, West End, early 1930s, a scene that is scarcely imaginable today. Regarded as the back of beyond by many people in Hayes, much of Yeading was covered by brickfields, which in turn became rubbish dumps. Since the First World War housing has now largely taken over the area.

The Industry Inn, Yeading Lane. Located just south of the bridge over the Yeading Brook, this was one of the three public houses that served the area in the early years of the twentieth century. Brickfield and agricultural workers were probably the main customers, although it may have been considered to be a cut above the others as a desirable inn on the road to Hayes Town and Botwell. The original Industry, seen above, was replaced by the current building between the wars.

The Walnut Tree, Yeading. This public house in Willow Tree Lane was built in about 1840 when a tenant landlord was hard to find because of the poor road communications at the time. This building was replaced in 1929 by the present pub.

Yeading chapel. This small building was opened as a Mission Hall on 5 January 1902 in memory of Mr Charles Horace Harcourt. It was sponsored by Baptist and Methodist tradesmen from Ealing. In the 1920s it was bought by Mr W.J. Newbould of Hayes Baptist church, who held an afternoon Sunday school there. By 1942 it had become Yeading Baptist church, and by the 1980s had become the Hayes Apostolic Protestant church.

Yeading Manor Farm. This house was the successor, in 1848, to an earlier building on the site. It was a fairly typical Victorian house, built of brick with a low pitched slate roof. There are records of the manor of Yeading, a sub-manor of Hayes, going back to 1307, when it belonged to Walter, Bishop of Lichfield and Coventry, but in 1848 it was owned by the Revd John Louis Petit, whose Yeading Manor Farm coat of arms and the date appear over the front door of the house. Below is the farmyard behind the house. At the left is the granary, dated 1767, and further away to the right is the farmhouse. The splendid barn, nearly 110 ft long, would have been behind the photographer on the north side of the farmyard. The farm buildings, together with the house, were demolished in about 1962 to make way for the housing estate at Larch Crescent.

St Christopher's School, Uxbridge Road. Top: general view. Bottom: the courtyard. This large building, which stood in the Uxbridge Road on the corner of Coldharbour Lane, was opened in 1901 as an industrial school for delinquent Jewish boys. It was among the first establishments of its kind to train boys for a skilled occupation after release, and instruction was given in woodwork and metalwork, together with school lessons and physical training. Lord Rothschild donated £6,000 towards the cost of the school, and the bulk of the rest of the money came from the Jewish community. Jewish boys were not, it seems, in the majority, and while religious teaching was the responsibility of the superintendent (Mr I. Ellis, from the school's beginnings until the 1930s), according to one of the pupils the entire teaching staff were members of the Church of England; all apparently worked together harmoniously. The Hayes Certified Industrial School for Jewish Boys was eventually renamed St Christopher's. Following a new concept in the care of young persons it was demolished and replaced by the St Christopher's Community House on a nearby site – the first of its kind in the country.

Townfield Senior School, *c.* 1932. This view shows the girls' school on the left and, further away, the boys' school on the right. The building of the UDC housing estate of over 1,700 houses moved the population centre of Hayes to the north, and a large site on the estate was allocated for schools. The senior school was built by local builders W.S. Try, of Cowley, and officially opened on 18 February 1932. The Clayton Road School was closed and many of the teaching staff moved to the Townfield site, which closed as a school in 1987 and is now the Hayes campus of Uxbridge College.

Townfield School Orchestra, December 1933. Note the presence of both girls and boys.

Toilet Block, Coldharbour Lane. When in 1956 the Local History Society decided to build up its photographic collection of local buildings efforts were concentrated on the older and more important buildings and those at risk of demolition. It was realised also that a true record of the area should eventually cover at least typical examples of more mundane buildings; some of them ugly or uninspiring. A case in point was the public lavatory at the northern end of Coldharbour Lane. This modest building (number 3520) was added to the collection not long before it was demolished in the late 1990s.

Botwell was the scattered hamlet lying near to the railway station and canal in what is now the main shopping area of Hayes. This picture was taken in about 1913 in Golden Crescent (as it is now called). Botwell Mission Hall (built in 1910) shown on the left, is now incorporated into Hayes Public Library. The row of cottages is interesting in that weatherboarded extensions have been added at either end – probably after about 1790 when the brick tax made timber construction more economic. These cottages, and, needless to say, the well in the middle of the road, have now gone.

Canal Bridge, Station Road, Hayes, *c.* 1914. This is, strictly speaking, Botwell, although these buildings were not built until after the Grand Junction Canal was constructed in 1794. Then came the railway station, and most important, the factories from about 1900 onwards. The bridge is No. 200 on the Grand Junction (later Grand Union) Canal. The public house, the Old Crown, and the row of shops still exist, although much modern development, including tower blocks, has taken place in this area in recent years.

Hayes Station – then (as now) officially known as Hayes & Harlington – *c.* 1914. The station was opened in 1864, some twenty-five years after the neighbouring stations at Southall and West Drayton. A reminder of the old Great Western Railway's broad (7 ft) gauge, altered in 1892 to standard gauge, can be seen in the wide spacing between the two pairs of rails on the right. Sandow's Cocoa & Chocolate factory (later Nestlé) in the background is shown under construction (see next page). The adjacent site formed part of the National Filling Factory for wartime munitions production.

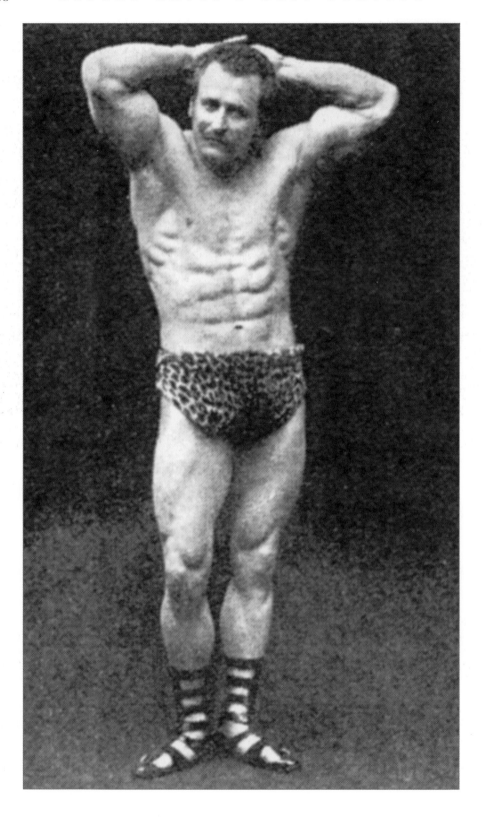

Nestlé's chocolate factory. This aerial view from the early 1930s shows the darker-coloured original Sandow's factory building with the major additions made by Nestlé around it. The factory had advantageous transport links to the railway and canal.

Opposite: Eugen Sandow. This remarkable man was responsible for the foundation of what became (and still is) one of the major industries in Hayes. He was born as Frederick Müller in Germany in 1867. After leaving school and university, he studied medicine, but then decided to become a professional strongman at the age of twenty. At this time he changed his name to Eugen (later, Eugene) Sandow. He toured Europe performing feats of strength in circuses and music halls, and in 1893 he went to America for two years. On one occasion he wrestled with a lion at a performance in San Francisco and won! As his active career as a strongman came to an end he became involved in physical culture and founded several academies of physical fitness and other associated enterprises in the United Kingdom, and in 1901 he became a British citizen. Convinced that cocoa contributed to health and strength he opened a cocoa processing factory in London. Wishing to expand, Sandow acquired a site in Hayes and built a factory that opened in 1914 as Sandow's Cocoa and Chocolate Co. Some years later the company went into liquidation and was renamed Hayes Cocoa Co. It was eventually taken over by Nestlé and greatly expanded to its present size.

The Army Motor Lorries & Waggon Co. Ltd, Clayton Road, Hayes, *c.* May 1915. This company was formed in England to build transport vehicles for the Belgian Army after most of Belgium had been occupied by the Germans. Shown in the foreground in the factory yard are two trailers for an automobile field hospital: one is an operating theatre with tent extensions, the other carries electric generators. Behind is a row of Lacre lorries with bridging pontoons on semi-trailers, and standing beside the corrugated iron shed are two Sheffield-Simplex armoured cars. The terrace of houses in Clayton Road shown in the background no longer exists, although the adjoining terrace (partly shown) is still standing.

National Filling Factory, No. 7, Hayes. This factory was one of a number built in 1915 at the instigation of Lloyd George, Minister of Munitions, to augment the supplies of artillery shells for the army. It occupied a large site south of the railway, almost down to where the M4 motorway at Cranford is now. The sheds were widely separated and connected by wooden walk-ways to lessen the risk of a major explosion. The site was chosen by Mr A.C. Blyth, who later became the factory manager. Construction was by the contractors, Higgs & Hill Ltd, and began on 18 September 1915, and the filling of shells in the factory began on 30 October 1915. Some 12,000 people, 10,000 of them women, were employed there. Two years later, on 23 October 1917, a serious accident occurred when many women workers were killed or injured.

National Aero Engine Factory, 1918, was another factory in Hayes dedicated to the war effort in the First World War. Aeroplane engines were manufactured there from about 1917 to the end of the war. The building in Blyth Road was originally completed by 1904 for Goss Printing Press Ltd, who were still there in 1913. From about 1922 to 1927 the factory was used for the manufacture of cars and lorries by the McCurd Lorry Manufacturing Co. Ltd, which had the proud slogan 'Thought out first – not found out afterwards'.

Fairey Aviation Co.'s works, North Hyde Road. Fairey were building aircraft at premises in Clayton Road, Hayes, in 1915, but after their main works were established in North Hyde Road, just in Harlington, they retained Hayes as their postal address. Some of the earliest aircraft designed by Fairey were flown from the field behind the factory. Above are the works entrance and main offices in 1918. Fairey were taken over in 1960 by Westland Aircraft Ltd, who closed the North Hyde Road works in 1972. The site is now an industrial estate.

Cartridge Case Inspection Department of the Gramophone Co., 1916. The outbreak of war in 1914 coincided with the opening of the company's new gramophone factory. The company had little option but to suspend its plans for expansion, but was able to survive by securing a contract for making munitions. As a direct consequence employment at Hayes increased four-fold; most of the employees, as seen here, were women, many of whom had previously been in domestic service. In 1939 the company, by now EMI, was once again employed in war work. This continued after the war with a significant proportion of the company's work being obtained from defence contracts. The end of the cold war and the collapse in the market for records in favour of compact discs was largely responsible for the demise of the company's operations in Hayes.

Opposite, below: Original factory buildings of the Gramophone Co., Blyth Road, 1969. The Gramophone Co. was founded in 1898 and opened the record factory seen here in 1907. The company gradually extended its activities and became better known by its trade mark His Master's Voice (HMV). After a merger with the Columbia Gramophone Co. in 1932 it became EMI, although the HMV record shops retain the original name. Records continued to be made by EMI in Hayes, although on a very much reduced scale, until 2000. The buildings seen here were scheduled for demolition in 2001 as part of the redevelopment of the EMI factory complex that at one time had employed 17,000 people.

Premises of the Vocalion Gramophone Co., Silverdale Road, 1969. The Aeolian Co. came to Hayes in 1909 and opened a factory in Silverdale Road for the manufacture of mechanical pianos. The premises were gradually extended, and by the early 1920s the company had diversified into making gramophones and gramophone records under the name of the Vocalion Gramophone Co.. The company went bankrupt in 1932 and their factory buildings (most of which still exist), were taken over by other companies. Ironically, the record factory was later used by EMI, its older and more powerful rival. This building was demolished soon after the photograph was taken.

Aerial view of the EMI factory complex, early 1950s. The EMI factories occupy the centre of the photograph. To the north a great deal of open land still remained, and part of this has now become the Lake Farm open space that is being developed as a country park. The railway line cuts across the bottom third of the picture and to the south of this are the premises of what was then the Fairey Aviation Co. (see page 31).

2

Harlington

Harlington in 1865 from the 6 miles to 1 inch Ordnance Survey Map. The map shows the middle two-thirds of the parish, the missing parts are the Dawley area in the north and a small triangular section in the south. Fruit orchards surround the village High Street; at this time much of the area around Harlington and Sipson was given over to intensive fruit growing (see pages 99 and 112).

Aerial view of Harlington and Sipson, on a bright sunny day in July 1996, shows Harlington just to the right of centre and Sipson on the extreme left. The M4 motorway and Airport Spur Road had been opened only two years earlier and represent ugly scars on the remnants of the agricultural landscape. In 1966 much of the field pattern imposed by the Harlington Inclosure Award of 1821 still remained, but this has since been almost totally obscured by gravel excavation. The land around the villages is still, in 2001, part of the metropolitan green belt, which has preserved most of it from building, however, hardly any has escaped the ravages of gravel companies. The existence of so much open land to the north of the airport has not escaped the covetous gaze of the civil aviation Mafia which on several occasions has proposed that it would be an ideal site for a third runway at Heathrow. If this were ever to be built it would follow the line of Sipson Lane and Cranford Lane that run roughly parallel to the M4 and A4 in the middle of the picture.

Station Road, looking north from just outside Bedwell House, *c.* 1910. All the houses still exist, but they have lost their neat iron railings and front garden walls. This part of Harlington is usually regarded as being in Hayes, but in fact the boundary between the two goes as far north as North Hyde Road. Before Hayes & Harlington station opened in 1864 the road was known as Bedwell Lane.

Dawley Road, *c.* 1930. Looking north from outside the Great Western. All of Dawley Road is in Harlington, after it joins North Hyde Road at Bourne's Bridge, the road as it continues northwards, forms the boundary between Harlington and Hayes.

Dawley House, *c.* 1925. This building, which had been the dairy of the palatial Dawley House, was all that remained after the main buildings were demolished in the late eighteenth century. It inherited the name of its more illustrious predecessor, and with the rest of the Dawley estate, was acquired by the De Salis family who sold it to the Gramophone Co. (EMI) in 1929. It was pulled down by the company in the early 1950s.

Dawley Wall, 1970. The long wall which runs along the western edge of Dawley Road is all that remains of the large Dawley estate. It dates from the mid-eighteenth century when the Earl of Uxbridge was lord of the manor of Dawley. Tradition relates that he had it built to keep out the plague, but many large estates have similar walls around them where they border a public highway. Much of the wall is in a ruinous condition, but parts have been restored to form the boundary of Stockley Park.

The Church of SS Peter and Paul, Harlington, *c.* 1878. The noticeboard outside the church misleadingly gives 1086 as the date of the foundation of the church, but this is merely the date of the Domesday Survey, which states that there was a priest at Harlington, but makes no mention of a church. In fact a church on this site probably existed long before 1086, but none of this building survives. The earliest part of the present church is the south wall of the nave and the doorway that dates from the twelfth century. This is the earliest known photograph of the church and shows that, except for the tower, the flint rubble walls were covered with plaster until the restoration of 1880. On the extreme left, the famous yew tree can just be seen (see page 43).

Church Porch and Church Farm, *c.* 1930. The porch around the twelfth-century doorway dates from the sixteenth century. It does not quite fit over the doorway, which suggests that it was not made on the site and was possibly taken from another church. Church Farm (see page 42) stood opposite the church gate, and was demolished in 1969.

Bennet Monument, Harlington church. The first member of the Bennet family to own Dawley was Sir John Bennet (I) (died 1627), who purchased the manor together with that of Harlington in 1607. Members of the family continued as lords of both manors until 1724 when Charles Bennet, who by then had become the Earl of Tankerville, sold them to Henry St John, Viscount Bolingbroke. Several members of the family are buried beneath the floor of the church, but the only readily visible indication is the monument, shown here, to Sir John Bennet (III) (1616–94). He was created Baron Ossulstone in 1682, taking his title from one of the Hundreds of Middlesex. In 1686 he had a monument erected to himself and his first and second wives inside the church. This monument depicts Sir John in the centre and his wives on either side. The date on the monument suggests that he must have died in 1686 and that both wives had predeceased him. In fact he founded a charity for apprenticing poor boys of Harlington in 1691 and the Harlington Burial Registers record his death on 11 February 1694/95. The registers record the burial of his second wife Bridget on 21 July 1703. Sir Henry Bennet (1618–85), perhaps the best known of the family, was the younger brother of Sir John. He was created an earl in 1672 and chose to take the name of the parish where he had lived as a boy. Through an error in transcription he became the Earl of Arlington.

Opposite, below: The site of the rectory gardens during the course of the redevelopment, as seen from the church tower. In the extreme left corner is the new rectory that was the first of the new buildings to be erected. In the background is the Moats recreation ground before the many elm trees were killed by Dutch elm disease. The name is derived from a medieval moat that existed on the land until it was filled in during the 1930s. The recreation ground was given to Harlington in 1938 by Ada Philp in memory of her father Sam Philp (1859–1936), and part of the bequest was that it should be known as the Sam Philp Recreation Ground, although the older name survives as an alternative.

Parts of the old rectory on the north side of the parish church dated from the sixteenth century, but the main front part shown above was an attractive Victorian building, The rectory was demolished in 1970 and most of the trees cut down to make way for a housing site that has done much damage to the former peaceful and attractive setting of the ancient parish church.

Hector Reindorp, Rector of Harlington 1932–47 at the ordination of his son, George Reindorp, as Bishop of Guildford 1961. Left to right: George Reindorp, Geoffrey Fisher (Archbishop of Canterbury) and Hector Reindorp. George later went on to be Bishop of Salisbury (1973–81).

The rear view of Church Farm from a painting by F. Griffith, 1937 (see also page 39). As its name suggests the farmhouse stood immediately opposite the church. It was a T-shaped, timber-framed house with a brick front that had been added in the eighteenth century. It became unoccupied in the mid-1960s, and as a result of extensive vandalism it had to be demolished in 1969.

The Harlington Yew Tree, 1770. The yew that stands to the south of the church porch is a now a very insignificant feature, but 200 years ago it was the subject of much comment because of the topiary work that formed part of the annual village fair held at Whitsun. The illustration is from a print published in 1770 by William Cottrell, the parish clerk from 1754–77, with a rhyme by John Saxy, described in the parish registers as a gardener, who died in 1741. It is clear from the rhyme that Saxy was responsible for clipping the tree, and it is probable that this was continued by Cottrell and his son, William, who succeeded his father as parish clerk. After the death of William Cottrell (II) in 1825 the clipping ceased and the tree reverted to its natural shape; it was severely damaged by a gale in 1959.

The trunk of the Harlington Yew, 1999. After it was damaged in 1959 the tree made a remarkable recovery. It has suffered from subsequent high winds, but although only a shadow of its former self, it has a healthy appearance and is growing vigorously. The photograph shows the extent of the trunk and the damage it has suffered over the years. As the rhyme in the previous picture relates even in 1729 'within 'tis true she's not so sound but hollow from the top to ground'. The bole of any yew tree presents the appearance not of a single trunk but several trunks that have coalesced, and this appearance is very marked in the case of the Harlington Yew. This condition is due to the yew continually pushing out new shoots from the lower part of its bole, which then coalesce with the old wood. This explains the longevity of yew trees and why the Harlington Yew has been able to recover repeatedly from damage that would have killed most other species. In 1990 a survey of ancient yew trees by the Conservation Foundation estimated that, using all the data it had to hand, the Harlington Yew could well be over 1,000 years old.

Dawley Manor Farm was one of the oldest (sixteenth century) and most attractive of the farmhouses that stood in the village High Street. The top illustration is from a painting commissioned in 1940 when it was feared that the house would be demolished to allow for the widening of the High Street. It survived for another twenty-two years, but was directly in the line of the M4 motorway, and was therefore demolished when construction started in 1962. The peaceful scene below, from about 1935, is now part of the busiest section of the M4.

Jessop's Pond, *c.* 1910. This pond was just to the north of Dawley Manor Farm and took its name from Joseph Jessop who owned the farm in the early nineteenth century. The M4 motorway now occupies the foreground and the fire station the woodland on the right to the north of the pond. The pond formed part of Frog's Ditch that rises in the Pinkwell area, runs through the Moats and along Watery Lane, after which it joins the River Crane. Most of the stream has now been culverted.

Watery Lane, 1991. Until the M4 motorway was constructed in the early 1960s this lane presented a pleasant walk from Harlington High Street to Cranford Park. It still leads to the park, but much of it was realigned when the M4 was built. Some of the old lane survives and still looks very pleasant in the spring. However, in reality the deafening roar of the adjacent motorway completely destroys any illusion of a rural scene.

Cherry Lane, *c.* 1930. The lane led from Harlington to West Drayton, and here is the beginning of the lane at its junction with the High Street almost opposite Dawley Manor Farm. On the right is Moat Cottage, built in 1910, which takes its name from the adjoining field that contained a moat that possibly surrounded the Harlington manor house. On the left are the extensively wooded grounds of Harlington Rectory. In 1962 the M4 motorway cut Cherry Lane in half, and the fragment seen here became a cul-de-sac that was renamed St Paul's Close.

Here is the lane in 1959, near the point where it was soon to be cut in half by the M4. At that time babies being pushed in prams by their mothers for a walk were still a common feature. Now, because of the traffic, it would be impossible to push such a baby carriage, and these have disappeared from the scene to be replaced by collapsible pushchairs that can be easily folded to go in a car boot.

Frogsditch Farm, Shepiston (formerly Cherry) Lane, 1969. This farm is named after the stream that runs nearby. In 1969 it was owned by F.W. Longhurst who had previously had a farm at Heathrow before he was evicted in 1944. After his retirement most of the farmland was acquired by gravel companies and has since been dug for gravel, although admittedly it has been well restored. Most of the farm buildings remain, but they have been badly affected by various unauthorised commercial uses completely incompatible with a green belt designation.

Bletchmore and Veysey's Farm, just before demolition in 1970. Harlington High Street was once lined by substantial houses belonging to the local farmers. All stood in large gardens, and, in consequence, most have been demolished and the gardens turned into small housing developments. Bletchmore and Veysey's Farm were typical examples; the former only dated from the early 1900s, but Veysey's Farm was about 100 years older. The farmhouse had presumably at one time belonged to the man who gave it its name, but nothing is known of him.

High Street, northern end, *c.* 1920, from a point opposite to Bletchmore, and about 150 yards south of the church, which can just be seen above the roof of Pear Tree Cottage on the left. Earlier photographs show it as a thatched cottage. It was pulled down in the 1930s. The iron railings on the left belonged to Vine House (see below).

Vine House and Philp's baker's shop, early 1900s. The house had been occupied by the Philp family who had farmed in Harlington for several hundred years. The baker's shop had been in existence as such since the mid-nineteenth century. The buildings were pulled down in the early 1960s and the site is now occupied by flats numbered 120–30 High Street.

High Street at the junction with Victoria Lane. This view of the northern end of the village, taken from the corner of Brickfields Lane looking north is from a postcard dated 1904. The buildings in the picture are Rose Cottages, pulled down in 1960; the house known as The Cottage, demolished in 1977 and sandwiched between this and Vine House, were the premises of Philp's bakery (see previous page).

The White Hart c. 1930. According to a plaque on the wall, the main part of the present building that stands at the junction of the High Street with Victoria Lane, dates from 1810, although the name is much older than this. The extension on the right was built in the 1920s; a further similar extension was added in the 1970s.

Victoria Lane, *c.* 1930, taken from the opposite side of the High Street. Victoria Lane was designated as Private Road No. 4 in the Harlington Inclosure Award of 1821. It may pre-date the inclosure, but it was clearly intended by the Inclosure Commissioners to provide access to the newly enclosed fields on either side. By the mid-nineteenth century it had become White Hart Lane; it did not become Victoria Lane until well into the reign of Queen Victoria. The roofs of the two sets of cottages at the end of the lane can just be seen (see below).

Cottages, Victoria Lane, 1970. Until the modern houses were built in 1956–7 these two sets of three cottages were the only houses in the lane. The curiously named Bet Linge Cottages (nearest the camera) were built in 1899, and were presumably named after the owner. The white rendered Victoria Cottages are some fifty years older; they do not appear on the 1821 Inclosure Map, but are marked on the Tithe Map of 1839.

Shackle's House, which appears to have had no name other than that of its last owners, stood on the east side of the High Street opposite the White Hart. It dated from the very early nineteenth century, was of yellow brick construction and had a slate roof. A wing was added on the north side later in the century. The house was demolished in 1960 and the flats in Pembury Court were built on the site.

Woodlands, *c.* 1920. This former farmhouse stood on the west side of the High Street, south of the White Hart. It was demolished in 1960, but one of the farm's barns survives as garages to the houses built on the site. It was brick built with a tiled roof, gabled at one end and half-hipped where it faced the road. Although the house had eighteenth-century features it could well have been much older.

The National School, High Street, *c.* 1920. Harlington and Cranford National School was opened in 1848 by the church authorities of the two parishes. It stood on the east side of the High Street on the site now occupied by old people's bungalows (249–63 High Street). It was closed in July 1939 and the children were transferred to the newly opened William Byrd School on the Bath Road. The school was then used for industrial purposes until it was demolished in the early 1960s.

Red Lion crossroads, *c.* 1920. This view of the High Street looking north shows the Red Lion on the extreme right and in the middle distance the barn belonging to Woodlands (see page 52). Both of these buildings remain, but all the others have gone. The white building on the left is Gothic House that had been converted into one large house from a row of cottages. It was demolished in the early 1960s and replaced by the houses in Gothic Court.

The village centre, *c.* 1905, shows the Baptist church on the right, which is the only building in the picture still left standing. The village pond (Butt's Pond) in the left foreground was still a proper pond, but with the urbanisation of the area the water level dropped, until by the 1950s it held water only during wet periods. In 1961 it was filled in, grassed over and planted with trees to become what is apparently the village green. The parish pound, with its railings and hedge, is the circular enclosure just behind the pond. To the left of this is Chapel Row and behind the pound is Manor Farm, the site of which is now occupied by the shops in Manor Parade. A plaque in the area of the pound records 'This area was once the VILLAGE POND AND ANIMAL POUND. It was landscaped to commemorate the QUEEN'S SILVER JUBILEE IN 1977.'

The barn at Manor Farm. The farm was demolished in the 1930s to make way for the shops in Manor Parade. All that was left of the farm was an eighteenth-century barn that stood just to the south of the farmhouse. Although the internal timbers of the barn were in good condition the exterior was in a ruinous state. Because the barn was on a list of local buildings of historic interest it had some protection against demolition, and therefore a developer converted it to office accommodation while retaining the roof timbers.

Baptist Lecture Hall, pre-1880, before the addition of side extensions. The original building dates from 1770, and it has been added to at various dates since then; the dissenting group meeting there became Baptists in 1798. In 1857 it was described as 'the ugliest building in the village', but by modern standards it is one of the more interesting features. In 1879 the new Baptist church was built and the old building used for meetings and lectures, hence its name. It was renovated in 1975 and renamed the Frank Peace Hall, but has since reverted to its old name.

Baptist church and manse, *c.* 1920. After extending their old building on many occasions, the Baptists ran out of space and built a new church on the other side of the road in 1879. The foundation stone on the corner records that it was laid by Thomas Wild (see page 56). The Grade II listed building with its classical frontage makes it, after the parish church, the most important building in Harlington. The building on the left, partly obscured by trees, was the late eighteenth-century Poplar House that was sadly demolished to make way for Felbridge Court in the 1960s.

Thomas Wild (1809–83) and his wife Mary Ann (1818–98). Thomas Wild originated from Sipson, where, until very recently, the family had farmed for several hundred years. In his later years he came to live at The Lilacs (see below). Like most of his family he played a prominent role in the non-conformist churches in the area, and he laid the foundation stone of the new Baptist church in 1879. His wife Mary Ann (née Cooper) was born at Sipson House (see page 113), and her brother married Mary Ann Mitton who was the inspiration for Charles Dickens's Little Dorrit.

The houses behind the pond, 1967, just after the pond had been filled in and just before The Lilacs, on the extreme left, was demolished. The other buildings are the early eighteenth-century Cedar Cottages and the old Baptist church. The Lilacs was renamed when Thomas Wild became the owner. Before that it had been known as Overberg House and was a private school. The house was reputedly the home of William Byrd, the Elizabethan composer, who lived in Harlington from 1577 to 1592.

The south end of the village. This view of the village High Street dates from the early part of the twentieth century, and was taken from a point just outside the Wheatsheaf looking south towards the Bath Road. The smaller building on the right was F.H. Bond's grocery store, which, as can be seen from the lettering on the wall, also sold china and glass. It no longer exists, but the larger building beyond it still contains shops. On the left in the middle distance is a terrace of houses known as Sunnyside Cottages, that was demolished in 1958 and replaced by a terrace of the same name. All that can be seen of Ferris's butcher's shop on the extreme left is the covered area of the doorway.

This view, dating from the 1920s, was taken from the opposite direction to that above, with the large building on the right above now on the left and advertising Evans Clothing and Outfitter. In the distance on the right the roof of the Baptist church can just be seen. The cottages on the extreme left stood on the corner of West End Lane and were demolished in the 1930s.

The Dower House, *c.* 1890. The front part seen here was built in the early sixteenth century; a wing extending to the rear was added later in the same century. It is a timber-framed building, to which the brick front was added in the eighteenth century. Apart from the parish church it is probably the oldest building in Harlington.

The Coach and Horses. This old eighteenth-century coaching inn stood at Harlington Corner for nearly 200 years giving pleasure to many and offence to none until it was quite needlessly destroyed when the Ariel Hotel (now the Post House Hotel) was built in 1961. The view, dating from the early 1900s, is to the east; on the extreme right Malmesbury Cottages can just be seen.

The Pheasant. When these photographs were taken the hamlet of West End was separated from Harlington by the length of West End Lane. The Pheasant, which dates from the mid-eighteenth century, was the first building to be met on the way from Harlington. The elm trees on the north side of the lane have long since disappeared to be replaced by houses in The Crescent. The Pheasant itself has changed little in the intervening years. Below is a scene outside the Pheasant in the early twentieth century.

Ploughing match, Harlington, 1935. The Middlesex Agricultural and Growers Association held its annual ploughing match in the Heathrow area in the early autumn. This is the ninety-seventh match. The champion ploughman in the foreground with two horses abreast ploughing with iron ploughs was Mr A. Prosser of W. & S. Philip & Son, Harlington, who is on the right of this photograph. He won it again at the ninety-ninth match in 1937 which was the last ever to be held; a drought in 1938 caused the postponement of the 100th match and the outbreak of war in the following year sounded the death knell. On his grave A. Prosser, who died in 1980, is recorded as the last champion ploughman of Middlesex.

Opposite, above: Bath Road, Harlington, *c.* 1910, looking west from a point about 100 yards east of the junction with New Road. On the left are Pomona Place, Oddfellows Cottages, the police station, Daisybank and Fern Villas. All except the police station were demolished in the early 1950s. The police station was moved to West Drayton in 1965 and the building was subsequently demolished. Derby Cottages are on the right.

Opposite, below: Snow scene, Sipson Lane, *c.* 1910. This view looking east was taken about 100 yards from the Harlington, Harmondsworth and Cranford Cottage Hospital which is the only building to be seen. Heavy falls of snow in the winter frequently blocked local roads as the occasional horse-drawn carts using the road would have done little to help clear the snow. The situation was worsened by the hedges on either side of the road acting as a snow fence in reverse as they trapped any snow drifting off the adjacent fields. The hospital was erected as a joint venture by the three parish councils in 1884. Extensions at the rear of the building were added in the 1920s and the operating theatre, which formed part of the extensions, was built as a memorial to the men of Harlington killed in the First World War. The hospital was closed in 1974, and it was later sold to the Sant Nirankari Mandal Universal Brotherhood.

The River Crane at the Cranford end of Cranford Lane, with Cranford Bridge carrying the Bath Road over the river. This brick-built bridge of three arches was rebuilt in 1776 by the Brentford Turnpike Trust, and the Colnbrook Turnpike Trust paid them £29 12s for making up the abutment on the Harlington side. The bridge was completely rebuilt again in 1913 and widened in 1960. The two people in the photograph are Mrs Shackle of Harlington and one of her sons.

The River Crane and Cranford Lane, c. 1920. This is the view that can still be seen on leaving Cranford High Street and heading towards Harlington. For a short distance the lane follows the river before turning sharp left and crossing the river over a narrow hump-backed bridge. The above view was taken from the near bank of the river but looking back in the opposite direction towards the Bath Road.

3

West Drayton

Empire Day on West Drayton Green, 1913. Maypole dancing on the green was a familiar sight on May Day and Empire Day in the early part of the twentieth century and was watched by the whole village. Behind the trees on the left stood the Copse (see page 69) and Switzerland House, which has also disappeared. The Foresters public house is no longer licensed and the building has been converted into two flats, but its title survives in the name of the house that has been erected behind it. The Cash Stores was destroyed by fire in 1934 and was later rebuilt. Maypole dancing was last held on the green in the early 1930s.

Drayton Hall. This much-restored early nineteenth-century building was the home of the De Burgh family, Lords of the manor of West Drayton. It was here that Hubert De Burgh entertained his friend, Napoleon III, ex-emperor of the French, in 1872. Napoleon Cottages in Money Lane are named after him. A bell plaque bearing the words 'Napoleon's Room' has survived from the former servants' quarters. After the death of Hubert De Burgh the mansion was let to various tenants. During the First World War it was occupied by a girls' school that had been evacuated from Paris. Later it became a private hotel. In 1948 the Yiewsley & West Drayton UDC was given permission to purchase the hall for £10,000 and to convert it into council offices. Under the London Borough of Hillingdon, it continued to be used as local government offices until 1986. In 1988 it was acquired by a developer and sympathetically restored for use as commercial offices.

Opposite, below: Weir Cottage. This small, thatched bungalow stood on the peninsula opposite West Drayton Mill and was used as a fishing lodge by the De Burgh family. Later it was occupied by Mrs Bazeley who bred blue Persian cats there, one of which was the champion of the National Cat Show at Crystal Palace in 1929. In 1942 the bungalow was destroyed by fire. A modern bungalow and dog kennels now occupy the site.

West Drayton Mill. A water mill existed at West Drayton at the time of the Domesday Survey, and by 1559 two wheat mills and a malt mill were housed under the same roof. Towards the end of the seventeenth century a paper miller, Nicholas Falcon, became the lessee, but corn milling was continued for many years. A century later Nicholas Mercer, mealman and paper maker, acquired the mill and rebuilt the whole complex, including the Mill House. By 1833 there were two millboard mills in operation, and in 1876 West Drayton Mill was described as the largest millboard mill in existence. In 1893 the Mercer family disposed of its interest in the mill to the West Drayton Millboard Co. Ltd, which was soon producing twenty tons of cardboard for bookbinding each week and employing forty local men. A succession of fires occurred at the mill at the end of the nineteenth century, and in the early twentieth century; one in 1904 caused damage estimated at £10,000. A more disastrous fire in February 1913 gutted the building.

Cottages on West Drayton Green shortly before they were demolished to make way for the building of Daisy Villas in 1896. During the hungry forties of the nineteenth century many Irish immigrants settled in West Drayton, and some of them occupied these cottages. There was much overcrowding, as many as twenty-five being recorded as living in one of the cottages, which were known locally as the Irish hovels.

A group outside Southlands. In the early twentieth century Southlands, an eighteenth-century house was occupied by the author Cosmo Hamilton and his actress wife, Beryl Faber, sister of Sir C. Aubrey Smith. This photograph was used by the Hamiltons as a Christmas card in 1906 and shows them outside the house with their pony and trap.

St Catherine's Roman Catholic church was built in 1869 to meet the religious needs of the Irish immigrants who had settled in the district following the Irish potato famine. Next to it stands Rumble's Bakery, established by Amos Rumble in 1875. To the right of this is the Crown Inn.

The Crown Inn, West Drayton Green, c. 1895. The earliest reference to the Crown is in 1689. The meeting to receive objections to claims made under the Inclosure Act was held here on 23 July 1824. The inn closed in 1924 and the bakery that stood next door was replaced by a new shop on the site of the old inn. The man standing centre right holding the hand of his daughter, Grace, is the landlord, Albert Edward Starnes.

West Drayton Green, *c.* 1900. On the extreme left in the foreground can be seen a corner of a building that was built in 1807 as the parish workhouse. It was later used for many years as a butcher's shop. On the east side of the green are the village shop and post office (see below); some nineteenth-century cottages; the Brewery Tap, adjacent to the Britannia Brewery; the King's Head; and Elmsdale, an early eighteenth-century house with an interesting portico.

The old post office, the green. Built in the seventeenth century, this building became the village shop and post office. Records show that in the early eighteenth century the churchwardens bought rope here for the bells of St Martin's church. In 1766 the business was bought by John Haynes who paid £26 0s 10¼d for the stock in trade and the fixtures. The original inventory shows the variety of goods on sale: 'Cheese, flower, mops, womens pattens and clogs, treacle, ginger bread, candles and powder and shot'. A small brewhouse was at the back of the premises. The business was carried on by John Haynes's descendants until shortly after the Second World War. The shop continued under various owners until 1972 when the premises were converted into a private residence.

The Copse was a delightful Tudor farmhouse that stood on the corner of the green and Money Lane. It had been refaced in brick and had a late eighteenth-century addition fronting Money Lane. Until 1919 it had been the home of the Batt family, who were farmers in West Drayton for many generations. It later became a private hotel, and in the 1930s was a private school, Heathlands Copse. The Copse was demolished in 1966 and a block of flats now occupies the site.

The old Swan public house was demolished in 1964 and its successor was opened the following year. The adjoining seventeenth-century cottages were demolished under a slum clearance order a quarter of a century earlier.

Swains in Swan Road. In all probability the house took its name from a family living in the district in the seventeenth and eighteenth centuries, one of whom, Thomas Swain of Harmondsworth, cast a bell for St Martin's church in 1770, for which he was paid £18 6s 5d. Records show that the house existed by the mid-seventeenth century, but much of it was altered or rebuilt in the eighteenth and nineteenth centuries. In recent years most of its garden has been sold for development, and in 1968 the oldest part of the house was demolished to make way for road improvements. West Drayton Baptist church, built in 1925 at a cost of just over £2,000, now occupies the site of the tree in the foreground.

Drayton House, known earlier as Burroughs, was a Tudor mansion standing on the west side of Swan Road. Its extensive grounds covered the whole of the area between Swan Road and Colham Mill Road. In 1923 the estate was sold by auction to a developer for £9,000. The mansion was demolished and a new road constructed in the middle of the grounds was named Ferrers Avenue after Earl Ferrers, a former owner, who bought the estate for £503 in 1785. When the house was demolished the ornamental eighteenth-century wrought-iron gates were sold for £200 and are now at Oxhey Grange, near Bushey.

West Drayton National School. The school that occupied the site of the present West Drayton Library was built in 1859. Its first master and mistress, Mr and Mrs Styles, lived in the schoolhouse and received a joint salary of £60 p.a. The schoolhouse was demolished in 1939 when Station Road was widened, and the building ceased to be used as a school in 1946. The old school building was demolished in 1962 and its name plaque has been incorporated into a wall of the library.

Children at West Drayton National School, 1901. Several photographs of the pupils exist from the early 1900s. The little girl with long hair sitting in the middle of the front row is Gertrude Starnes; none of the others can be identified.

The Closes. The path between the avenue of elms is thought to follow an old Roman trackway that ran from St Albans to Staines. At one time the trees continued in an unbroken line from St Martin's church, West Drayton, to St Mary's church, Harmondsworth, but in the early years of the twentieth century those in the southern part were felled and the path extended only to Laurel Lane, part of a housing estate built in the early 1950s. The remaining trees fell victim to Dutch Elm disease and were felled in 1975. Efforts to replace them have only recently shown signs of success.

The blacksmith's shop, West Drayton, 1923. The era of the blacksmith declined with the advent of the motor car, but at the time of the 1861 census there were no fewer than five men in West Drayton who worked at the anvil. Among them was Alfred Brown who lodged at the Crown Inn.

St Martin's church choir, c. 1914. Seated in the centre is the vicar of West Drayton, the Revd A.W.S.A. Row, who was the incumbent from 1889 until his retirement in 1928. Standing behind him is the choirmaster, Mr W.J.R. Ratcliff.

The ivy-mantled tower of St Martin's church before its restoration in 1926. By then the ivy had caused the tower to crumble. It became dangerous and consequently it was necessary to close the tower entrance and to place a fence around the structure. An appeal was launched for £1,175 to restore the tower, plus a further £425 to repair and rehang the bells. The tower was restored, and in 1932 the tenor bell was recast and rehung. The remaining bells of the peal remain unhung, as the depression of the 1930s prevented sufficient funds being raised for their restoration.

The interior of St Martin's parish church showing the Victorian pews and pulpit, which dated back to the restoration of 1850–2. The Ten Commandments above the chancel arch were painted over in 1931. In 1974–5 the church underwent a major restoration. It was completely refurnished and the altar was placed at the western end. The total cost of all this work was £43,000. Sadly none of the remaining bells has been rehung.

The old St Martin's vicarage, *c.* 1905. The rear part of the vicarage was built in the seventeenth century, probably as a farmhouse. The main block on the right was added in the mid-eighteenth century, while the large block on the left was a much later addition. The house was acquired for use as a vicarage on 24 May 1888 at a cost of £720. It remained the official vicarage until 1960 when the present vicarage was erected in its grounds. The old vicarage was demolished in 1963 and St Martin's Hall now stands on its site. The vicar, the Revd A.W.S.A. Row and his family are shown above. Later the vicar moved to the Gate House and let the vicarage, which was then renamed the Grange. At the beginning of his ministry there were no motor cars and the penny farthing bicycle could be seen locally. By the time he retired the age of the aeroplane had arrived.

Church Lane (now Church Road), early 1900s. The entrance to the road from West Drayton Green is shown. On the left is the sixteenth-century boundary wall of the former manor house and on the opposite side of the road are some nineteenth-century cottages that were demolished during the slum clearance scheme of the 1930s.

Church Lane. A view from the front door of the Aspens looking north along Church Road. On the left is the boundary wall that surrounded the Paget manor house of about 1550, and in the background are the Victorian houses shown opposite at the top of page 77.

Higher up Church Road these large, red-brick houses stood on the right-hand side. They were built in 1881 and were mainly occupied by professional people who could afford to employ servants. In the days before piped water the supply to these houses came from a pump in the kitchen, and one of these pumps has been preserved. After the financial crisis of the 1930s most of the houses were let as flats. They were demolished in 1975 and Shawfield Court flats were erected on the site.

Bagley Close, *c.* 1930. This is a short cul-de-sac leading from Church Road with bungalows built in the 1920s. The close is named after the Bagley family who farmed in the district in the nineteenth century.

The Aspens, Church Road. A house stood on this site in 1824, which was then in the possession of the Jacquet family. By 1871 the building shown here was occupied by the Thatcher family who owned the Britannia Brewery on the Green. In the 1920s it was purchased by R. Colboys-Wood who ran a horticultural business from there, transforming the garden and fields into a magnificent advertisement for his wares (see page 76). The house was badly damaged by fire in the 1930s and demolished in 1939.

Station Road, West Drayton, 1920s, before it was widened in 1939–40. On the left is Mr F.S. Collard's Parade Garage, and on the right is his cycle shop. Just visible beyond the garage is the corner of Mr Luther Rix's newsagent's shop. Next is the lock-up fish and chip shop owned by Mr Richardson, while the other shop on the left with the gabled roof is Bellclose Dairies. All the buildings on the left were demolished during the road widening, but those on the right, known as the Parade and built in 1908, still remain. Next to Collard's cycle shop is Mr Masters's grocery. Yiewsley telephone exchange occupied the next shop until the present telephone exchange next to the post office was opened in 1937, when the exchange was renamed West Drayton. The next shop was Mr Batten's greengrocery and the final shop was a draper's owned by Miss Belch.

West Drayton and Yiewsley West signal box. There had been two signal boxes at West Drayton since the new station was opened in 1879, the west box controlling the junction of the branch lines to Uxbridge and Staines, as well as the main lines to the west. The west box as rebuilt is shown above in March 1912. It remained in use until 16 May 1960.

Batt's Corner. The road from West Drayton to Sipson on the left and to Harmondsworth on the right as it appeared until the mid-1930s. The wooden boundary fence of Drayton Hall can be seen on the right, while the Fox and Pheasant (formerly the Cherry Tree) public house now stands on the left. The spinney is now a parade of shops known as Dell Corner. This is probably the most altered part of West Drayton, the junction being controlled by traffic lights.

Riverside scenes, 1923 and 2001. Harmondsworth Moor is crossed by several branches of the River Colne, the third of these, along Moor Lane, is the Wraysbury River. One of the attractive features of the moor was the riverside walk from Harmondsworth to West Drayton. On the left, at one of the idyllic spots along the walk, are Arthur Perryman and his nephew by marriage, Herbert Ferguson, seated at a spot where all is now desolation. Just beyond, the M4 motorway now crosses the river and the riverbank is occupied by lines of vehicles from a nearby breaker's yard (below) which is seemingly allowed to operate with impunity in what is part of the Colne Valley Regional Park.

4

Yiewsley

High Street, Yiewsley, from Colham Bridge, before 1905, the year that Barclays Bank moved to its present site. When the bank moved a drapery business, owned by the Misses Adams, occupied the shop. The old Anchor and the blacksmith's shop are shown on the left and then Clayton's butcher's and greengrocery shop. In the middle is the Red Cow public house that was rebuilt in 1962. Note the absence of traffic.

The northern end of Yiewsley High Street facing towards Uxbridge as it appeared in the early years of the twentieth century. To the left is Trout Road and Falling Lane is to the right. The northbound road has been widened and a large roundabout constructed at the crossroads. The ivy-covered house, once known as Straw Farm, has given way to offices and a motor showroom stands opposite, on the corner of Falling Lane.

The badly sited Colham Bridge at the end of Yiewsley High Street before it was rebuilt in 1939. Johnson's Wax factory was opened in 1919 in the former Colham Wharf (built in 1796). The wax factory remained on this site until it was transferred to another district in 1960. It then had 350 on the payroll.

Colham House Bakery. In 1904 the Collins brothers transferred their bakery and catering business from Belsize Park, Hampstead, to Colham House, which stood on the old Colham Bridge over the canal. This was a high-class bakery and dairy business that included catering facilities. The business closed when the canal bridge was rebuilt in 1939.

The old Anchor public house. The pub, now renamed Bentleys, was rebuilt in 1939 on an adjacent site when Colham Bridge was reconstructed. Next to it stood the blacksmith's shop – one of many in the district, but now extinct.

The old Red Cow occupied an important and extensive site in the High Street. On one side was a large beer garden and on the other were outbuildings and a yard on which stood a greengrocery and fruit stall. In the early years of the century the yard was the venue of street entertainers and cheapjacks on a Saturday night. The old inn was demolished and the whole site developed in 1962. The modern Red Cow stands on the beer garden of its predecessor.

Coach outing from the Brickmakers Arms in Horton Bridge Road, Yiewsley. The pub took its name from its customers who worked in the Yiewsley brickfields. It provided a social centre for the Horton Road area of the village, and numerous outings in horse-drawn vehicles were organised for its customers. The photograph shows one of these outings with the licensee, Mr Tom Belsey, wearing a bowler hat, seated at the top left-hand corner with his wife on his left. Tom Belsey died in 1931 after having held the licence for 33 years 8 months. It was during the early part of his tenancy that the inn was rebuilt.

Left: Smith & Haynes ironmongery shop, 113 High Street, the building to the left of the cottage, 1881. The business was established in the year of the photograph, and until 1982 it occupied its original site with a modern shop built on the front garden of the cottage above. The premises have since been converted into a restaurant.

The Otter Dock ran from the canal through the grass centre of the present Colham Avenue and beyond to the brickfields. As the brickfields became worked out, traffic through the dock ceased and it became a dumping ground for rubbish and decaying vegetable matter. After prolonged disputes between Yiewsley Parish Council and Uxbridge Rural District Council work started on filling in the dock in 1909. In 1904 the road on the west side of the dock, then known locally as Dock Road or Wharf Road, was renamed Colham Road. The road on the east side was Ernest Road. After the dock had been filled and the area had been grassed over they became one road, but the separate names continued until 1938 when the road was renamed Colham Avenue.

The Floating School, Yiewsley. This was provided by the Grand Union Canal Co. for the children who lived on barges travelling along the canal and also for use as a mission boat for canal workers. It was named Elsdale after a benefactor of canal boatmen, and was dedicated by the bishop of Bermuda at Paddington Basin on 29 September 1930 before being brought to Clayton's Wharf. It had accommodation for forty pupils, and it was estimated that 100 children would attend the school each week. The barge school remained at Yiewsley until 1939 when it was transferred to Bulls Bridge, Southall.

Padcroft College opened on 4 October 1875 in Padcroft House, Yiewsley, which stood on the site of the present Heathcote Way flats. Its principal was the Revd G.H. Jones, and its syllabus claimed that by giving a liberal English education it prepared its pupils for public schools, the professions and commercial life. Its fees were 2 guineas per quarter for day boys or 40 guineas per annum inclusive for boarders. At one period it could claim 100 pupils on its roll, and in 1881 there were 16 passes in the Cambridge local and other

examinations. The college prospered under the Revd G.H. Jones, but there were financial difficulties under his successor, Mr E.J. Allen (1884–7). Under its last principal, Mr W.H. Birkett, who purchased it in 1887, Padcroft College regained much of its original renown. The college closed in the early years of the twentieth century.

Padcroft Boys' Home. After Padcroft College had closed the building was acquired as a boys' home by the Church of England Temperance Society in 1902. Later it was transferred to the London Police Court Mission. Padcroft Boys' Home continued until 1949, and during the whole of its existence had but one manager, Mr F.A. Green. During that period great emphasis was placed on sport and athletics.

Harmondsworth and Longford, 1966. This view, taken on a bright sunny day in July, shows Harmondsworth village almost in the centre and still mostly surrounded by fields. The ugly scars caused by the gravel workings in the north-west corner can be seen clearly, and these were soon to engulf Harmondsworth Moor. Halfway across the bottom quadrant is the Y-junction formed by the Bath Road and Colnbrook bypass with the Old Bath Road and Longford straggling to the extreme south-west. In 1966 the main northern runway at Heathrow had yet to be extended up to the edge of Longford village. To the east the fields between Harmondsworth and Sipson are still largely intact, but the ominous scar just to the south of the M4 motorway are a portent of things to come.

This photographic tour of the large parish of Harmondsworth starts in Harmondsworth village, continues via Harmondsworth Lane to Sipson and thence along Sipson Road to its junction with the Bath Road at the Magpies. After a short diversion along Heathrow Road to Heathrow it returns to the Bath Road and continues to the western extremity of the parish at Longford.

5

Harmondsworth – Sipson, Longford & Heathrow

Oak Cottages occupied a prominent position on the south side of the village street at its junction with Summerhouse Lane. The right-hand cottage was built in the early part of the sixteenth century, the other two were rebuilt at a later date. In 1933 the cottages were included in a proposed slum clearance order, and there was an immediate outcry against the suggested demolition. As a result of strong pressure from the Society for the Preservation of Ancient Monuments and the National Trust the cottages were withdrawn temporarily from the scheme. Efforts were made to raise funds for their preservation, including an appeal in *The Times*, but these proved unsuccessful. The clearance order was reimposed late in 1935 and the cottages were demolished in November 1937.

The Great Barn. The top illustration shows a print of the barn from 1793, and below it is shown on an open day in 1993 from the top of the church tower. The Great Barn, often incorrectly known as the Tithe Barn, is one of the finest medieval barns in England and dates from about 1450. Although not, as claimed in this old print, the largest in the kingdom, it is immense, being 191 ft long, 38 ft wide and 39 ft high. Externally it is impressive on account of its bulk, but the drawing does not give any indication of its magnificent interior that has been likened to a cathedral in wood (see facing page).

Interior of the Great Barn from a drawing by G.K. Welater. The print dates from 1880, but it still gives an accurate impression of the magnificent interior. Until 1970 the barn was still in agricultural use, but since then it has been restored to form part of the Manor Farm complex. The fact that it is a Grade I listed building, a scheduled ancient monument and adjacent to a twelfth-century church has not prevented civil aviation interests from identifying its site and that of the church as part of a third runway for Heathrow Airport.

St Mary's church, from a print dated 1793. This is one of the earliest depictions of the church. The view towards the south-east shows a turret on the north-west corner of the tower, which has since been removed and been replaced by a cupola (see below). Otherwise few changes have been made in the external appearance of the church. As can be seen below trees now obscure much of the view so that only the tower can be seen.

This view of St Mary's has changed remarkably little since the early 1900s. The only changes are that the Sun public house on the right is now a private house known as Sun House, and the Five Bells used to belong to Harman's (Uxbridge) Brewery until it was taken over in the early 1960s.

The Five Bells and church. This recent view shows how little the scene has changed in the past 100 years.

Harmondsworth Hall in Summerhouse Lane. The exterior of the house and fine doorway suggests a Georgian building, but it is much older, having been remodelled in the eighteenth century. It stands opposite The Grange, and like its neighbour originally had a large garden that ran for the length of Summerhouse Lane. Originally a private residence it is now a small hotel.

The Grange, 1937. The handsome red-brick house in Summerhouse Lane was built in 1675. This view shows the south side of the building, and between the two upstairs windows is a large wooden sundial which bore the date 1695. Soon after the photograph was taken, the sundial was sold at auction for £1 7s 6d. The house became dilapidated during the 1950s, but has been excellently restored to provide office accommodation. It has since been renamed, for reasons best known to the developers, as Harvard House.

Cambridge House, rear view at the turn of the nineteenth century. After The Grange and Harmondsworth Hall, this was the third largest house in the centre of the village, but unlike its neighbours, which only lost their large gardens, it was demolished in 1955 to make way for the houses in Cambridge Close. It stood in its own grounds next to the Crown.

Harmondsworth Baptist church. The present Baptist church on the corner of Hatch Lane and the Village High Street was erected after the original church had been destroyed in the fire that ravaged Harmondsworth in 1884. The buildings on the left and in the distance, the Five Bells, still survive. On the right is the Vicarage Hall (demolished in 1972), next to which is Blacksmiths' Row (demolished in 1938).

Village High Street, *c.* 1920. This view looking east shows the former Vicarage Hall on the extreme left and Blacksmiths' Row (now demolished). In the middle distance is The Lodge which was given a new lease of life following its restoration in 1978. On the right are Oak Cottages (see page 89), the Crown public house and next to this can be seen the gateway to Cambridge House, which was demolished in the early 1950s.

Duke's Bridge in Moor Lane crosses the Duke of Northumberland's River, an artificial watercourse cut in or about 1543 to divert water from the Colne to provide additional water supplies to Isleworth Mill (owned by the duke). The view is from the west bank of the river looking eastwards along Moor Lane.

Manor Farm 1993. This view was taken from the church tower at an open day at the church and Great Barn. Until the 1970s both the farmhouse and barn were part of a working farm, but the complex was then taken over by a building firm. This firm, in return for receiving planning permission to use the farmhouse for office accommodation, agreed to restore both the house and barn. This was very well done and the area, now known as Manor Court, is an excellent example of what can be achieved with a sensitive approach to restoration. The farmhouse dates from the early nineteenth century and occupies the site of the former manor House. At the extreme top, above the farmhouse, is an area of land which has since become the site of British Airways's Head Office, which cynics believe is intended to become Terminal 6 if permission for a third runway (which is being strongly advocated by British Airways) for Heathrow were ever to be granted.

Children of Harmondsworth School outside the Great Barn, 1904. The Harmondsworth School Log Book for 1904 records 'school closed today on account of the Annual Treat,' but then goes on to say 'the Treat has been postponed until tomorrow owing to wet weather.' The following day it records 'the Treat has taken place today in beautiful weather. A very enjoyable day was spent.' The date of the photograph and the fact that the Annual Treat did not take place, as was usual, suggests that it was taken at the barn. Of the children, only Arthur Perryman, the boy on the extreme right of the front row, can be identified. The schoolmaster on the right is probably, the headmaster, Mr Ward.

Harmondsworth School. The old village school was on the south side of Moor Lane, and the buildings remained as a clinic and meals centre until it was converted into what is now Old School House with the adjacent Moor House in the 1990s. On 4 November 1907 the school transferred to a new building backing on to the recreation ground, and this remained its home until the opening of the present Harmondsworth Primary School in January 1976. Later that year the 1907 building was opened as the Village Hall. Above are the gardens adjoining the Moor Lane School with the boys under the supervision of a master, probably Mr Ward, working on the land. The cottages in the background were demolished in the 1950s.

Houses in Moor Lane, *c.* 1930. The south side of Moor Lane from the village halfway to Duke's Bridge was lined with houses, many of considerable age. They were mostly in very poor condition, and one elderly resident recalls that as she walked down Moor Lane the smell from them was appalling. Above are the houses nearest to the village centre, and below is a rear view of some of the houses nearer to Duke's Bridge. All of the houses in both views, except two in the distance above, were demolished in the early 1930s as part of a slum clearance scheme. The houses that have replaced the old buildings were built at the rear of the former houses. When they were completed the old ones were knocked down and families moved from the old to the new.

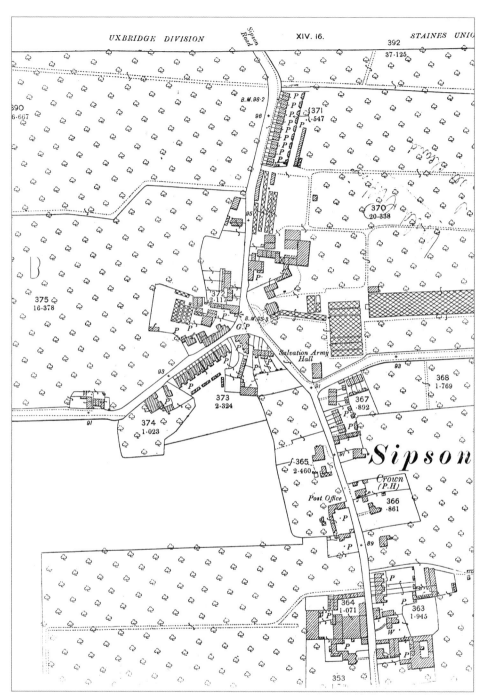

Sipson Village, 1895. This Ordnance Survey map shows the centre of the village where the roads from Harlington to the east (Sipson Lane) and Harmondsworth to the west (Harmondsworth Lane) join the village High Street. As the map shows, at that time orchards surrounded the village that was in the middle of a large fruit-growing area that covered much of south-west Middlesex. Within a few years most of the orchards disappeared to make way for intensive market gardening.

Heathrow Airport under construction, 1954. The airport appears as an ugly scar on the landscape to the south of the Bath Road. To the north of the road are the still relatively peaceful villages of Sipson, straggling linearly along Sipson Road on the left, and the nuclear village of Harmondsworth in the lower right-hand corner. The villages at that time were still surrounded by well-tilled fields in use for intensive market gardening. Within fifteen years most of this landscape had been destroyed by the construction of the M4 and the associated link road to the airport and by gravel excavations.

Harmondsworth Lane was the approach to Sipson, with Cedar Cottages on the right and in the middle distance The Vineries (see page 104). The cottages were owned by the Rayner family of The Cedars, Colnbrook – hence the name. However, they were much better known as the Sixteen Row, derived from the fact that there were four blocks of four terraced houses. They were demolished in the mid-1960s, and their bricks were used to build Nos 1–15 Harmondsworth Lane on the same site.

The village centre, at the junction of Sipson Lane and the High Street, 1967. From the extreme right to left is the corner of the Baptist church, The Vineries, the Coffee Tavern, Centre House, the King William and 394–408 Sipson Road. Centre House, the white building at the far end of the road, had been at one time Appleton's baker's shop and later a butcher's shop. It was then used by a firm of airport caterers until it was demolished in the 1970s. All the other buildings to the left of this still remain.

The King William, c. 1930. The King William occupies a prominent site in the centre of Sipson. This photograph gives a good impression of its medieval origins, but these have now been masked by a facelift carried out in the 1930s; more recently it has suffered the indignity of being converted into a Hungry Horse restaurant. It is in fact an unusual example for west Middlesex of a Weald-type hall house from the fifteenth century. The high-pitched roof suggests that originally it would have been thatched.

Vinery Cottages in Sipson Road at the northern extremity of the village. These cottages were built by Thomas Wild (see page 104) for his farm workers in 1888 and derived their name from The Vineries where he lived. Because there were nine pairs of cottages they were known locally as the Eighteen Row. The two pairs of cottages at the far end were badly damaged by a bomb in October 1940, so they were knocked down. The remainder were demolished in the early 1960s, and Nos 241–65 Sipson Road were erected on the site.

The Welcome Coffee Tavern. The members of the Wild and Robbins families were staunch non-conformists, and to discourage their workmen from drinking, the Welcome Coffee Tavern was opened in 1897 as a counter-attraction to the public houses. Non-alcoholic drinks could be obtained in the coffee room on the left and the reading room on the right was available as a recreational room in which to read, play games and pass the time of day. The tavern closed in the 1940s and was converted into a pair of semi-detached houses, these were needlessly demolished in 1983, since when the site has remained vacant.

Sipson Gardens. Top: *c*. 1910, bottom: 1979. This eighteenth-century building, which stood at the junction of Harmondsworth Lane and Sipson Road, was one of the few Grade II listed buildings in Sipson. Despite its listing, the roof, doors and windows were removed in the autumn of 1979 (as shown below), and no action was taken by Hillingdon Council to prevent this. Permission was subsequently given by the council for its complete demolition. In recompense a replica building was erected close to the original site, which has as much value compared with the original building as a mock antique does to the genuine article. Up to the early 1900s the house had been the home of the Appleton family who owned a good deal of property in Sipson. It was purchased from the Appletons by Charles Ashby and renamed Sipson Gardens. Prior to this the house had no proper name and was known merely as Appleton's house.

Left: Thomas Wild (1848–1932). *Below*: The Vineries, *c*. 1910. Until very recently, the Wild family had lived in Sipson for more than 300 years. At the turn of the twentieth century various branches of the family were farming in the area, the most successful business being Thomas Wild & Son of Sipson. In 1898 Thomas Wild took a junior partner, Rowland Robbins, to form the firm of Wild & Robbins. This firm owned much of the land and most of the houses in Sipson and dominated the life of the village. Thomas Wild, who had lived in an old house known as Sipson Farm, had the Victorian house shown below built for him. It stood in the High Street opposite the junction with Harmondsworth Lane and was pulled down in 1970. The houses in Vineries Close now occupy the site.

Right: Rowland Richard Robbins (1873–1960).
Below: Hollycroft, rear view, *c.* 1930.

R.R. Robbins was in all but name the senior partner of Wild and Robbins. He was created CBE for his services to agriculture in 1920, and was a man of considerable national importance in agriculture in the first half of the twentieth century. He rose to become the President of the National Farmer's Union, which was an incredible achievement for a Middlesex market gardener. On moving to Sipson he first lived in the old farmhouse that had been the ancestral home of the Wilds. It was here that his elder son, Lionel, was born, who was later to become Lord Robbins, and who chaired the Robbins Committee that recommended the expansion of university education in the early 1960s. In 1906 R.R. Robbins moved from Sipson Farm to Hollycroft, an early nineteenth-century house in the village High Street, and this remained his home until he severed his links with the Wild family and moved from Sipson in the late 1940s. The house was pulled down in the 1960s.

Top: Sipson Baptist church after its conversion from a gospel mission hall. The mission hall was built in 1891 at the instigation of Thomas Wild. For the first few years the Salvation Army was responsible for running the hall, and it is marked as such on the map on page 99. In 1897 it became a gospel mission and was enlarged to its present size in 1901. In 1905 the membership of the gospel mission formed themselves into a Baptist church. *Bottom*: Sipson Baptist church after its redevelopment in 1988. With Baptist churches close at hand at Harlington and Harmondsworth, the large church in Sipson became far too big to support a small and declining congregation. Therefore, the main part of the building was tastefully converted into flats (known as Church Court) and the church relocated in what had been the former Sunday school.

Sipson Mission Brass Band outside the Baptist church, *c.* 1905. Back row, left to right: A. Matson, Alf Thorn, Amos Perryman, and the band leader, Mr Wallace. Middle row: H. Williams, Fred Sansum, H. Howell, George Pearton Jnr, Jim Josey, Albert Whittington, John Dyble and Silas Perryman. Front row: J. Anders, George Pearton snr, J. Matson, W. Sansum and George Blay. On Sunday evenings the band used to play hymns before the service in various spots in the village.

Members of the Girls' Life Brigade outside the Baptist church, mid-1920s. In the first half of the twentieth century, and with the active participation of the Wild and Robbins families, the Baptist church was the focal point of social life in the village. Apart from the Sunday services and school, every night of the week was given over to some activity for the children. This included Band of Hope, where they were taught of the evils of drink, a Magic Lantern evening, a Boys' Brigade and, as shown here, a Girls' Life Brigade. The girls have not been positively identified, but the tall person in the middle of the back row is the Brigade Leader, Mrs Virtue.

Sipson post office and village stores, *c.* 1910. *Top*: the store is on the extreme left, in the middle distance is the faint outline of the Baptist church, and on the extreme right the front façade of the Crown can just be seen. At the time James Tyler was the proprietor of the shop that has been the village stores since at least 1830. The front part, seen here. is a Victorian addition, but the back is much older and is probably the oldest remaining building in Sipson. *Bottom*: the rear of the store with Henry Tyler, the father of the owner, with his tricycle outside the back door on 2 October 1911. This view of the house is still identifiable, although the bay window has since been removed.

The southern end of the village High Street, *c.* 1910. The top photograph, looking south, shows Gladstone Terrace (*c.* 1880), now 415–23 Sipson Road, on the left, and Holly Cottages, built in 1906, and named after Hollycroft, the home of R.R. Robbins, on the right. All the other buildings have gone; in the far distance on the left side of the road is Smith's Jam factory. Below, taken from the same vantage point, is the view in the opposite direction; most of the buildings still remain. On the left are Holly Cottages, now Nos 432–50 Sipson Road. On the right in the middle distance is the Crown, and the Baptist church is in the far distance.

Leek planting at Sipson Farm, *c.* 1950. The leeks were fed into the machine that was capable of planting three rows at a time. The operator facing backwards (Len Emery) is doling out the leeks to the three men (right to left Messrs Summerfield, Cowan and Pert) who placed the leeks between the jaws on a continuous belt that ran horizontally along in front of them. The jaws then closed and rotated through ninety degrees so that the leeks could be inserted into the soil. The Holiday Inn (formerly the Premier Post House Hotel) now stands on the area of planting.

A blacksmith's shop was part of the auxiliary activities of the firm of Wild & Robbins. It was used principally for their own benefit, but its services were available to others. Here is the blacksmith, Will Daniell, on the left, being assisted by Malcolm Wild, *c.* 1950.

Van works, Sipson Road, early 1900s. The blacksmith's shop opposite was part of a much larger complex that included what was known as the van works where Wild & Robbins made farm vehicles for their own use and for sale. Above is the inside of the works with some of the workmen and examples of some of the carts. Below, at a slightly later date, is one of the products that was clearly intended to be used by Thomas and Evans Welsh Hills Lemonade, Porth. The man standing proudly beside the van is the works foreman, F.M. Holman.

Factory and Registered Office:

SIPSON, MIDDLESEX.

T. A.: "SMITH, SIPSON RAILWAY STATION, WEST DRAYTON."

FRED^K SMITH'S FRESH FRUIT JAM

PRIZE MEDAL

RASPBERRY JAM
FRED^K SMITH
SIPSON
MIDDLESEX

FREDK. SMITH'S Exhibition Stand of Jams, Marmalade, Fruit Jellies and Bottled Fruits, which secured the Royal Horticultural Society's (Affiliated Societies) Premier Award, August 24th, 1907.

Sipson House, 1912, and the three eldest sons of H.E. Philp, who purchased the house in 1904. This fine Georgian house stayed in the Philp family until 1973 when it was bought by the British Airports Authority. BAA left it empty and did nothing to protect it from vandals. Hillingdon Council, with its customary lack of concern, also failed to demand that it should be kept in weather-proof condition. BAA sold it in 1979 and permission was given by the council to restore it and convert it to office use. This restoration took the form of total demolition of everything except the front façade so that the restored building is little more than a neo-Georgian replica.

Opposite: An advertisement for Smith's Jam (from *Kelly's Directory of Middlesex*, 1908). As the centre of a large fruit-growing area, Sipson was well placed to support a jam factory. Jonathan Smith, who owned many of the orchards in the area, opened the factory in the 1890s. At the time of this advertisement his son Frederick was the proprietor of the factory, who is standing on the left, with his factory foreman, Irons, who is on the right. The factory closed in the early 1920s and was partially burnt down in mysterious circumstances in 1943. The houses in Kenwood Close now occupy the site.

Sipson and Heathrow School, Bath Road, 1967. In 1874 the new Harmondsworth School Board decided to build a school for the children living in the eastern half of the parish. Until a site could be obtained and the school built, a temporary school was opened in Sipson House (see page 113). The school remained there until 1877 when it moved to the new premises, known initially as Heathrow School. When it was built it was about midway between the two hamlets, but Sipson expanded towards it, and as the majority of the children came from Sipson, it become Sipson & Heathrow School. The school closed in 1966 and was demolished in 1967. Its replacement in Harmondsworth Lane, Sipson, reverted to the original name of Heathrow School.

Empire Day, 24 May 1933. As with most schools across the country, the morning on Empire Day was given over to patriotic celebrations, followed by a half-day's holiday in the afternoon. Britannia is seated in the middle with groups of children around the flags of the four nations of the United Kingdom. In the centre foreground the Revd R. Ross, vicar of Harmondsworth, is addressing the children.

Sipson Corner, 1931. The roads to Sipson and Heathrow joined Bath Road at Sipson Corner in the area of Harmondsworth parish known as The Magpies (from the public house of that name). Above is the view to the east and the south side of Bath Road. During the 1920s a large number of transport cafés opened along most major roads of the country to cater for the increasing numbers of lorries. At that time they were not subject to planning controls and the standards of hygiene were poor. However, few were as bad as the café on the right, the site of which is now occupied by the airport police station. At the time it was known as Jock's Café, but soon after it was taken over by Ben Ward and renamed Ben's Café. Neither owned the freehold, which, sad to say, belonged to the author's great-uncle, Fred Cottrell. Unsightly advertising hoardings are on the right-hand side. The tramp on the left is crossing the junction between Sipson Road and Bath Road, a suicidal venture with today's traffic.

This view was clearly taken on the same occasion as the same lorry, which must have been stationary, appears in both photographs. This one, also looking east, shows the north side of the road and the junction with Sipson Road. Just beyond the junction is another café, but this was obviously catering for a superior clientele to that of its neighbour across the road.

The Bricklayers Arms, Bath Road, 1910. Master Reg Henley, who lived in a house next door, is standing between the licensee, Mrs Sturch, and her husband Thomas. The inn was demolished in 1928 so that Bath Road could be widened, and was replaced with a new Bricklayers Arms, which was renamed the Air Hostess in May 1954. For some years the licence was held by J.W. (Jack) Hearne, the well-known Middlesex and England cricketer, who died in 1965 at Bagley Close, West Drayton. The Air Hostess itself was demolished in the late 1980s and the site is now a drive-in McDonald's.

A scene outside the Old Magpies, 1951. The sixteenth-century coaching inn stood on the south side of Bath Road, about 100 yards to the west of the similarly named Three Magpies (a miraculous survivor of a bygone age). Both inns, on the edge of Hounslow Heath, were the haunts of highwaymen in the eighteenth century. The scene here shows the re-enactment of a hold-up outside the inn, which can just be seen in the background. It was held in 1951 on the last day of opening; the inn was demolished shortly afterwards. Hold-ups were, in reality, nothing like that seen here. In 1782 a Mr Mellish, brother of the MP for Grimsby, was shot and killed by two armed robbers outside the Old Magpies.

Heathrow Airport under construction, early 1950s. This view looking towards the west shows the runways virtually completed, with work just starting on the central terminal area. Work on the airport began in May 1944 under the pretext that it was urgently needed by the RAF. In fact, it was never used by the RAF and was intended, from the outset, to be a civil airport. The airport is shown as a cancerous growth on what is still basically a largely rural landscape. Like all cancers it has continued to spread and has engulfed most of the surrounding area.

The last day of the public inquiry into a fifth terminal at Heathrow, 1999. The inquiry began in May 1995 and ended on 17 March 1999 – the longest public inquiry on record. Its length was due to the strong opposition to the proposal; around 22,000 individuals and organisations made representations, of which 96 per cent were opposed to the development. On the right are some of the protestors outside the airport hotel where the inquiry was held.

NOTE.—The whole Freehold Estate as described in the following Particulars will first be offered in one Lot, and if not sold in its entirety will be withdrawn and submitted in the following Lots.

PARTICULARS.

LOT 1.

(Coloured pink on plan)

The Valuable and Important Freehold Property

KNOWN AS

HEATHROW FARM

Having a south aspect, and containing about

73 Acres, 0 Roods, 2 Poles,

Of very productive Arable and Pasture Land, possessing a total frontage of about 1,925 feet to Heathrow Road, comprising

A well-constructed old-fashioned brick-built Farm Residence, with tiled roof, which contains six Bedrooms, Drawing Room opening to Garden, Dining Room, Dairy, Kitchen, Scullery, Mangle Room; also an excellent supply of water and nice Garden, together with the extensive range of Farm Buildings, including three large Barns (two having tiled roofs, one corrugated iron), two Stables with six stalls each, Cow Lodge for 10 cows, Chaise House, excellent Granary, Implement Shed, Cart Shed, &c.

SCHEDULE.

No.					a.	r.	p.
84	House and Buildings	-		-	1	1	12
85	Garden	-	-	-	1	2	6
82	Orchard (part of)	-	-	-	0	3	2
83	Orchard	-	-	-	5	0	33
81	Pasture	-	-	-	2	0	13
98	Arable	-	-	-	62	0	16
					73	**0**	**2**

Held by Mr. Curtis with other lands under two separate leases, whereby he is now tenant from year to year until tenancy is determined by either lessee or lessor giving three years' notice in writing expiring on the 29th September in any year, at rentals amounting together to £258 per annum. The apportioned rental for this Lot shall be

PER £195 ANNUM.

Tenant paying all outgoings.

Sale details of Heathrow Farm. This farmhouse was situated on the north side of Heathrow Road just to the west of the Plough and Harrow (see opposite). It was a timber-framed building, dating from the late sixteenth century, that had been refaced with brick in the eighteenth century; it was demolished in 1944. Details of the farm are given in the particulars of the sale. These reveal that at the time of the sale, on 29 September 1906, the occupant's name was Curtis. The farm continued in the Curtis family until the family was evicted in 1944.

The Plough and Harrow, Heathrow Road, *c.* 1930. The only public house in Heathrow stood on the north side of Heathrow Road about ⅛ mile west of its junction with Cain's Lane. It dated from the mid-nineteenth century, and was demolished when the airport was developed in 1944.

Mr and Mrs Basham, the licensees of the Plough and Harrow, *c.* 1930. E.C. Basham was the landlord of the pub at the time. Prior to becoming the landlord Mr Basham had been a policeman. This and his appropriate name must have recommended him both to the police and to the licensing authorities.

Control tower at Heathrow. *Top*: 1946. An airport cannot operate without a control tower, so this was one of the first buildings to be erected. It was a crude brick box with direct access to Bath Road just to the north that stood roughly where the airport police station now stands. *Bottom*: The central control tower shortly after its completion, early 1950s. Designed by Frederick Gibberd and architecturally much superior to its predecessor, it has since been made a listed building.

Peggy Bedford was probably the best-known person in Longford during the first half of the nineteenth century. For over fifty years she was the licensee of the King's Head on Bath Road, and eventually the name of the inn was changed to that of its landlady. Peggy died on 2 February 1859, aged seventy-seven; her grave may be seen in Harmondsworth churchyard.

The Peggy Bedford, Longford, shortly before its demolition in 1993. This well-known landmark stood at the junction of the Old Bath Road and the Colnbrook Bypass. It was built to replace the old Peggy Bedford (see page 122) soon after the bypass was constructed in 1928. Had it been built a little further along the bypass it would probably have survived, but it occupied a prime location which made it an all too tempting site for a drive-in McDonald's.

The old Peggy Bedford, Longford (once the King's Head), standing behind two large elm trees, was a famous landmark on Bath Road. In 1859 the inn had stabling for eighteen horses and its gardens totalled over thirteen acres. The old Peggy Bedford was closed when the new inn was opened at the junction of Bath Road and the Colnbrook Bypass in 1928. In 1934 the old inn was partially destroyed by fire. The front part that had been completely destroyed was rebuilt and added to the surviving rear portion to form the large house known as The Stables.

College Farm, Longford, shortly before demolition. According to the Royal Commission on Historic Monuments this farmhouse dated from the seventeenth century. However, its name suggests that there may have been an older building of the same name on the site. The name was derived from the fact that from 1391 until 1543 the manor of Harmondsworth was owned by Winchester College.

The Square, Longford, *c.* 1900. Parts of the timber-framed White Horse on the right of the picture date from the sixteenth century, and it seems to have undergone some reconstruction 200 years later. The part of the village around the White Horse was known as The Square; just behind the public house is White's Farm. The bricked-up windows of the White Horse recall the window tax which was introduced in 1696 and not repealed until 1851.

The Barracks, Longford, 1990. This row of attractive cottages that runs in line from the White Horse is known as the Barracks. They possibly get their name from the fact that troops were billeted there during the Civil War. The cottages were later used to billet troops who were protecting the highway from robbers who frequented Bath Road during the stage coach era.

Pump on the Old Bath Road, near Mad Bridge, Longford, 1980. From 1727 until 1870 the Colnbrook Turnpike Trust had responsibility for the upkeep of Bath Road from Cranford Bridge to Maidenhead Bridge. The traffic using the road sent up a large amount of dust that made travelling very unpleasant, so the road was watered to keep the dust down. The Colnbrook Trust acquired a water cart in 1763, and in 1827 they erected fourteen pumps at intervals along the road for an outlay of £759. Until recently three of these remained, two being in Longford, but now only one survives outside the Punchbowl at Poyle. An erroneous inscription was added to this pump in the mid-1950s to the effect that it had been erected by order of Beau Nash of Bath in 1754. Apart from the fact that the erection of the pumps by the Turnpike Trust is well substantiated, by 1754 Nash was eighty years old, out of favour, living in poverty, and in no position to order the erection of the pumps. It is quite possible that Nash was responsible for the erection of pumps on the roads within the city of Bath, i.e. the Bath Roads not the Bath Road, and this is probably the origin of the error.

A view of Longford village taken from the King's Bridge looking eastwards, *c.* 1910. On the left is the porch of Zoar, later Zion, Baptist chapel, built in 1859. This still stands, although it is no longer used for worship. In the middle distance on the right is the King's Arms public house.

Colne Valley Meadow, Longford, 1999. Harmondsworth Moor and Longford Moor in the lower Colne Valley have been despoiled by gravel digging and airport-related developments. The meadow shown here is a unique survivor, and even more surprising is the survival of the hedge in the background, which is the ancient boundary hedge between the parishes of Harmondsworth and Stanwell, which must be several hundred years old. It is less than one mile from the end of the main runway at Heathrow, and its future is very uncertain.

5,000 people could be sent packing

Study looks at third runway

By Michelle Williams

TWO Hillingdon villages could be literally wiped off the map if plans to build a third runway at Heathrow Airport take off.

The proposal is being looked at as part of nationwide regional studies which will form the Government's Aviation White Paper for the next 30 years.

Part of the studies' brief is to look at if, and where, extra runways are needed in the South East to relieve congestion. Proposals would see the demolition of more than 3,500 homes in Sipson and Harmondsworth a mile north of the airport's boundary.

It would mean around 5,000 residents being forced to sell up and move, while the Grade I listed, 14th century tithe barn at Manor Farm, Moor Lane, Harmondsworth, would be demolished along with British Airways' £200m Waterside headquarters and the Government's immigration holding centre.

The new runway would be used by small and medium-sized short-haul aircraft, freeing-up around half the airport's present capacity. It would be around 70,000 feet long and roughly 40% shorter than the present two runways.

Department of Environment, Transport and Regions spokesman, Steve Warren, said those working on the studies, which began in March last year, had open minds about the proposal.

"A third runway is just one of options open to the study group which is looking at the best way to develop the aviation industry.

"Once the reports are complied and combined, whatever recommendations they make will be open to public consultation."

British Airways spokeswoman, Camilla Wrey, said other than being part of the working party putting together the white paper, the airline had no specific involvement in the proposal.

Airport operator BAA reconfirmed its position, taken during the T5 inquiry, that a third runway should not be considered by the Government.

Spokeswoman Cheryl Monk said: "In our evidence at the T5 inquiry we stated very clearly that BAA would support a recommendation to the government that it should rule out a third runway and invited the inquiry inspector to make such a recommendation."

Hayes and Harlington MP John McDonnell (Lab) said he would continue to fight the proposal as he had done for ten years.

"The third runway, along with T5, is clearly part of a long term strategy to develop Heathrow at any cost. They said there would be no T4 and look what they have got, just like they said there would be no T5 yet they came back for more.

"Now they're coming back for the third runway despite assurances this wouldn't be the case.

"Furthermore, this act of bad faith would not only devastate my constituency it would be an environmental nightmare."

Hillingdon Council leader and Greater London Assembly member Richard Barnes said the idea was a "complete no-go".

"The proposal for a third runway has been around for a long time but nothing has ever come of it. Can you imagine how much it would cost to buy out 3,500 homes all worth around £80,000 and upwards? And that's before the development has even started."

Hayes Gazette, 31 May 2000. Epitaph for Harmondsworth? As long ago as 1946 positive plans were made to construct a third runway at Heathrow, which would have involved the destruction of Harlington, Sipson and Harmondsworth. These proposals were abandoned in 1952, but are regularly resurrected from time to time. Even before the result of the inquiry into the fifth terminal was made known, the civil aviation Mafia began agitating for a third runway at Heathrow, as can be seen from this newspaper report. The current proposal would involve the destruction of Harmondsworth and Sipson, so that all the buildings depicted in this section, would be demolished. No doubt if they were to succeed there would soon be proposals to extend the runway and to demolish all the buildings in Harlington as well.

INDEX

ACKNOWLEDGEMENTS

Except where otherwise stated, all the photographs are from negatives or originals owned, either by the Hayes and Harlington Local History Society, the West Drayton and District Local History Society or P.T. Sherwood. Grateful thanks are due, however, to the various individuals who have donated or loaned, for copying, the original photographs, postcards and paintings, which have been reproduced. These include Mr J. Allport, Miss M. Bird, Major D. Francombe, Mr S.J. Heyward, Mrs N. Lee, Mrs R. McManus, Mr K.R. Pearce, Mr R. Robbins, Mr D.M. Rust, and Mr W.L. Wild.